Common Core
Standards Practice Workbook

Grade 3

Glenview, Illinois • Boston, Massachusetts
Chandler, Arizona • Upper Saddle River, New Jersey

ALWAYS LEARNING

PEARSON

ISBN-13: 978-0-328-75686-5
ISBN-10: 0-328-75686-5

8 9 10 V0N4 18 17 16 15

Grade 3 Contents

 **Standards Practice**

 **Assessment**

Pearson is pleased to offer this **Common Core Standards Practice Workbook**. In it, you will find pages to help you become good math thinkers and problem-solvers. It includes these pages:

- **Common Core Standards Practice pages.** For each Common Core Standard, you will find two pages of practice exercises. On these pages, you will find different kinds of exercises that are similar to the items expected to be on the end-of-year assessments you will be taking starting in 2014–2105. Some of the exercises will have more than one correct answer! Be sure to read each exercise carefully and be on the look-out for exercises that ask you to circle "all that apply" or "all that are correct." They will likely have more than one correct answer.

- **Practice for the Common Core Assessment.** You will find a practice assessment, similar to the Next Generation Assessment that you will be taking. The Practice End-of-Year Assessment has 40 items that are all aligned to the Common Core Standards for Mathematical Content. The two Performance Tasks focus on assessing the Standards for Mathematical Practice.

Name _____

Common Core Standards Practice

3.OA.A.1 Interpret products of whole numbers, e.g., interpret 5 × 7 as the total number of objects in 5 groups of 7 objects each.

1. Molly has 3 packs of pencils. Each pack holds 8 pencils. Molly writes 3 × 8 to represent the problem situation. What does 3 × 8 show?

2. There are 5 kittens. Each kitten has 4 legs. What expression can represent the total number of legs?

3. Write a problem story that matches 7 × 3.

4. Explain why your story matches 7 × 3.

5. Write a word problem story that matches 3 × 5.

6. Explain why your story matches 3 × 5.

7. Brad planted 6 rows of flowers. He planted 4 flowers in each row. Tell why 6 × 4 gives the total number of flowers Brad planted.

8. Marco buys 4 bags of apples. There are 10 apples in each bag. Tell why 4 × 10 gives the total number of apples.

3

Name _____

Common Core Standards Practice

3.OA.A.2 Interpret whole-number quotients of whole numbers, e.g., interpret 56 ÷ 8 as the number of objects in each share when 56 objects are partitioned equally into 8 shares, or as a number of shares when 56 objects are partitioned into equal shares of 8 objects each.

1. Sally is putting 32 muffins on 8 plates. Each plate has the same number of muffins. What expression shows how many muffins are on each plate?

2. Jon has 24 oranges. He puts 6 oranges in each bag. What expression shows how many bags John needs?

3. Write a problem story that matches 42 ÷ 7.

4. Explain why your problem matches 42 ÷ 7.

5. Write a problem story that matches 27 ÷ 3.

6. Explain why your problem story matches 27 ÷ 3.

7. There are 56 students sitting at 8 tables. Each table has the same number of students. What expression can tell the number of students at each table.

8. Ruben wants to buy 18 tennis balls. There are 3 balls in each can. What expression can tell the number of cans Ruben will need to buy?

CC 4

Name _____

Common Core Standards Practice

3.OA.A.3 Use multiplication and division within 100 to solve word problems in situations involving equal groups, arrays, and measurement quantities, e.g., by using drawings and equations with a symbol for the unknown number to represent the problem.

1. Hannah has 3 bags of marbles. In each bag are 6 marbles.

   a. Draw a picture to match to problem.

   b. How many marbles does Hannah have? _____

2. There are 16 stamps arranged into 4 equal rows.

   a. Draw an array to match the problem.

   b. How many stamps are in each row? _____

3. Five friends are at the school fair. They have 25 ride tickets that they will share evenly. Each friend gets the same number. For 3a–3d, choose Yes or No to indicate whether each number sentence could be used to find the number of tickets each friend gets.

   a. $25 \times 5 = \boxed{}$ YES   NO

   b. $25 \div 5 = \boxed{}$ YES   NO

   c. $5 \times \boxed{} = 25$ YES   NO

   d. $5 \div \boxed{} = 25$ YES   NO

4. Ms Donovan sets up her classroom with 4 rows of desks. Each row has 5 desks.

   a. Draw an array to show how many desks Mrs. Donovan has in her classroom.

   b. How many desks are there in all? _____

5. Sherri has 24 inches of yarn. She cuts the yarn into pieces that are each 6 inches long.

   a. Write an equation to show how many pieces of yarn Sherri has.

   _____

   b. How many pieces of yarn does Sherri have? _____

6. Roger's father has 6 pieces of wood. Each piece is 8 inches long. For 6a–6d, choose Yes or No to indicate whether each number sentence could be used to find how many inches of wood Roger's father has.

   a. $8 \times 6 = \boxed{}$ YES   NO

   b. $8 \div 6 = \boxed{}$ YES   NO

   c. $\boxed{} \times 6 = 8$ YES   NO

   d. $\boxed{} \div 6 = 8$ YES   NO

Common Core Standards Practice

3.OA.A.4 Determine the unknown whole number in a multiplication or division equation relating three whole numbers.

1. Write a multiplication number sentence to match this story problem.

Maddy needs to fill 6 baskets with canned goods for the food drive. She will put the same number of cans in each basket. She has 42 cans for the baskets. How many cans can she put in each basket?

Write the missing number in each number sentence.

2. _____ $\times\ 3 = 21$

3. $5 \times$ _____ $= 25$

4. $10 \times 1 =$ _____

5. $2 \times 4 =$ _____

6. $9 \times$ _____ $= 36$

7. _____ $\times\ 6 = 18$

8. For each expression in 8a–8d, answer Yes or No if the $\boxed{} = 4$ makes the number sentence true.

   a. $20 = \boxed{} \times 4$ YES   NO

   b. $8 \times \boxed{} = 32$ YES   NO

   c. $28 \div 7 = \boxed{}$ YES   NO

   d. $12 \div \boxed{} = 3$ YES   NO

CC 7

3

9. Explain how to use multiplication to find the missing number in this number sentence.

$$\boxed{} \div 6 = 7.$$

Write the missing number in each equation.

10. _____ ÷ 2 = 8

11. 7 ÷ _____ = 1

12. 35 ÷ 5 = _____

13. 80 ÷ 10 = _____

14. 9 ÷ _____ = 3

15. _____ ÷ 1 = 3

16. For each expression in 16a–16d, answer Yes or No if the $\boxed{}$ = 7 makes the number sentence true.

a. 56 = $\boxed{}$ × 8   YES   NO

b. $\boxed{}$ × 5 = 30   YES   NO

c. 63 ÷ 9 = $\boxed{}$ YES   NO

d. 24 ÷ $\boxed{}$ = 3   YES   NO

CC 8

Name _____

Common Core Standards Practice

3.OA.B.5 Apply properties of operations as strategies to multiply and divide.

1. For each expression in 1a–1d, answer Yes or No if the expression is equivalent to the product of 8 and 12.

   a. $8 \times (6 + 6)$ YES   NO

   b. $6 \times (8 + 6)$ YES   NO

   c. $(4 \times 2) + (6 \times 2)$ YES   NO

   d. $6 \times (4 + 4) + 6 \times (4 + 4)$ YES   NO

2. **a.** What is the missing number in the equation?

   $3 \times 10 = \underline{\hspace{1cm}} \times 3$

   b. Explain how you know.

3. **a.** What is one way to find $5 \times 2 \times 4$?

   b. What is another way to find $5 \times 2 \times 4$?

CC9

4. If you know that $5 \times 15 = 75$, how can you find 15×5?

5. You want to find $9 \times 2 \times 3$. Would you start by finding 9×2 or 2×3? Explain why.

6. Rosie wants to find 5×12. She breaks apart 12 into $10 + 2$. Then she writes $5 \times (10 + 2)$ as $(5 \times 10) + 2$.

   a. What mistake did Rosie make?

   b. What is 5×12? How do you know?

Name _____

Common Core Standards Practice

3.OA.B.6 Understand division as an unknown-factor problem.

Write a multiplication fact that can help you solve each division number sentence.

1. $12 \div 4 = ?$

2. $35 \div 7 = ?$

3. $7 \div 1 = ?$

4. $36 \div 6 = ?$

5. $25 \div 5 = ?$

6. $27 \div 3 = ?$

7. Which multiplication fact can you use to solve the division number sentence?

$14 \div 7 = \boxed{}$

A $7 \times 1 = 7$
B $7 \times 2 = 14$
C $2 \times 14 = 28$
D $7 \times 7 = 49$

CC 11

8. What multiplication fact can you use to find $72 \div 8$?

9. What multiplication fact can you use to find $48 \div 6$?

10. What are two division number sentences you could solve by using the multiplication fact $7 \times 3 = 21$?

11. What are two division number sentences you could solve by using the multiplication fact $4 \times 8 = 32$?

12. Which division number sentence can you solve using the multiplication fact $10 \times 2 = 20$?

    A $10 \div 2 = ?$

    B $20 \div 2 = ?$

    C $10 \div 5 = ?$

    D $20 \div 5 = ?$

CC 12

Name _____

Common Core Standards Practice

3.OA.C.7 Fluently multiply and divide within 100, using strategies such as the relationship between multiplication and division (e.g., knowing that $8 \times 5 = 40$, one knows $40 \div 5 = 8$) or properties of operations. By the end of Grade 3, know from memory all products of two one-digit numbers.

Solve.

1. $\begin{array}{r} 8 \\ \times\ 7 \\ \hline \end{array}$

2. $\begin{array}{r} 6 \\ \times\ 8 \\ \hline \end{array}$

3. $39 \div 3 = $ _____

4. $36 \div 9 = $ _____

5. $\begin{array}{r} 12 \\ \times\ 5 \\ \hline \end{array}$

6. $\begin{array}{r} 9 \\ \times\ 6 \\ \hline \end{array}$

7. $54 \div 6 = $ _____

8. $72 \div 8 = $ _____

9. $\begin{array}{r} 7 \\ \times\ 9 \\ \hline \end{array}$

10. $\begin{array}{r} 7 \\ \times\ 7 \\ \hline \end{array}$

11. $40 \div 5 = $ _____

12. $32 \div 4 = $ _____

CC 13

Solve.

13.
$$\begin{array}{r} 5 \\ \times\ 9 \\ \hline \end{array}$$

14.
$$\begin{array}{r} 7 \\ \times\ 4 \\ \hline \end{array}$$

15. $42 \div 6 = $ _____

16. $72 \div 6 = $ _____

17.
$$\begin{array}{r} 9 \\ \times\ 9 \\ \hline \end{array}$$

18.
$$\begin{array}{r} 12 \\ \times\ 8 \\ \hline \end{array}$$

19. $60 \div 5 = $ _____

20. $90 \div 9 = $ _____

21.
$$\begin{array}{r} 5 \\ \times\ 4 \\ \hline \end{array}$$

22.
$$\begin{array}{r} 11 \\ \times\ 6 \\ \hline \end{array}$$

23. $77 \div 11 = $ _____

24. $48 \div 4 = $ _____

CC 14

Name _____

Common Core Standards Practice

3.OA.D.8 Solve two-step word problems using the four operations. Represent these problems using equations with a letter standing for the unknown quantity. Assess the reasonableness of answers using mental computation and estimation strategies including rounding.

1. Jeremy bought 9 water bottles with a $20 bill. Each water bottle cost $2. How much change should Jeremy receive?

   a. Write an equation to match the problem. Use the letter *c* to stand for the missing number.

   b. Solve the problem. Explain how you found the answer.

2. Isabel and Hank build birdhouses. Isabel builds 3 birdhouses every day. Hank builds 2 birdhouses every day. How many birdhouses can they build in 5 days?

   a. Isabel says they can build 15 birdhouses in 5 days. Is her answer reasonable? Explain how you know.

   b. Write an equation to match the problem. Use the letter *b* to stand for the missing number.

   c. Solve the problem. Explain how you found the answer.

3. A box of light bulbs costs $5. Each box holds 4 light bulbs. How much money will Fran spend to buy 8 light bulbs?

   a. Write an equation to match the problem. Use the letter *m* to stand for the missing number.

   b. Solve the problem. Explain how you found the answer.

4. Jerome needs 65 balloons for a party. He already has 18 red balloons and 13 blue balloons. How many more balloons does Jerome need?

   a. Write an equation to match the problem. Use the letter *b* to stand for the missing number.

   b. Solve the problem. Explain how you found the answer.

   c. Explain how you could use an estimate to check that your answer is reasonable.

Name _____

Common Core Standards Practice

3.OA.D.9 Identify arithmetic patterns (including patterns in the addition table or multiplication table), and explain them using properties of operations.

1. Look at the numbers in the table. What pattern do you see?

2	5	8	11	14

Use the multiplication table for Problems 2 and 3.

X	0	1	2	3	4	5	6
0	0	0	0	0	0	0	0
1	0	1	2	3	4	5	6
2	0	2	4	6	8	10	12
3	0	3	6	9	12	15	18
4	0	4	8	12	16	20	24
5	0	5	10	15	20	25	30
6	0	6	12	18	24	30	36

2. Look at the row for 6 in the table. Explain why 6 times a number is always even.

3. Look at the row for 4 in the table. Explain why 4 times a number can be written as the sum of two equal addends.

4. Look at the numbers in the table. What pattern do you see?

7	14	21	28	35

Use the addition table for Problems 5 and 6.

+	1	2	3	4	5	6
1	2	3	4	5	6	7
2	3	4	5	6	7	8
3	4	5	6	7	8	9
4	5	6	7	8	9	10
5	6	7	8	9	10	11
6	7	8	9	10	11	12

5. Look at the row for 5 in the table. Explain why the numbers in this row follow the pattern even, odd, even, odd.

6. Explain why the sum of two equal addends is even.

Name _____

Common Core Standards Practice

3.NBT.A.1 Use place value understanding to round whole numbers to the nearest 10 or 100.

Round each number to the nearest ten.

1. 118

2. 731

3. 1,552

4. 2,219

5. 6,382

6. 925

7. Which of these numbers, when rounded to the nearest 10, is 780?
   Circle all that round to 780.

   784   789   773   776   758

8. Explain how to use place value to round 286 to the nearest 10.

Round each number to the nearest hundred.

9. 210

10. 2,547

11. 1,472

12. 889

13. 2,149

14. 7,975

15. Ryan says that 472 rounded to the nearest 10 is 500. Is Ryan correct? Explain.

16. Which of these is equal to 360? Circle all that are equal to 360.

4 × 90   80 × 4   12 × 30   40 × 9

50 × 7   6 × 60   40 × 8   5 × 60

Name _____

Common Core Standards Practice

3.NBT.A.2 Fluently add and subtract within 1000 using strategies and algorithms based on place value, properties of operations, and/or the relationship between addition and subtraction.

Add.

1.   237
       + 194

2.   359
       + 209

3.   808
       + 115

4.   556
       + 436

5. What is 438 + 194?

   A 522

   B 564

   C 622

   D 632

6. What is 703 + 167?

   A 800

   B 810

   C 860

   D 870

7. a. Find the sum. 243 + 239.

   b. Explain how you added 243 and 239.

Subtract.

8.   320
     − 16

9.   334
     − 53

10.   289
      − 122

11.   901
      − 576

12. What is 487 − 158?

    A 321

    B 329

    C 331

    D 339

13. What is 901 − 76?

    A 825

    B 835

    C 925

    D 975

14. Lilly says that 512 − 392 is 280.

    a. How can Lily use addition to check her answer?

    b. Explain how you know that Lily's answer is incorrect.

    c. What is the correct answer?

CC 22

Name _____

Common Core Standards Practice

3.NBT.A.3 Multiply one-digit whole numbers by multiples of 10 in the range 10–90 (e.g., 9 × 80, 5 × 60) using strategies based on place value and properties of operations.

Multiply.

1. $7 \times 20 =$ _____

2. $8 \times 40 =$ _____

3. $9 \times 60 =$ _____

4. $2 \times 30 =$ _____

5. $6 \times 70 =$ _____

6. $5 \times 50 =$ _____

7. Explain how you can use 4×4 to help you find 4×40.

8. To find 8×70, Nora first wrote 70 as 7×10. Explain why this step can help Nora solve the problem.

9. Write the factors in the matching column. Some factors may not belong in any of the columns.

360	480	180

6×80 80×2 4×90 12×40

30×6 60×6 8×40 2×90

CC 23

10. Match the factors with the products. Some products may have more than one set of factors. Some products may have no sets of factors.

3×70 80×3 5×50 12×20 40×6

210   240   250   270

11. A bookstore receives 7 boxes of books. Each box holds 20 books.

a. Write a multiplication fact that shows how many books there are in all.

b. Explain how you can use 7×2 to help solve the multiplication problem.

c. How many books are there in all?

12. Anna multiplied 2×50 and got 10.

a. Explain how you know that Anna's answer is incorrect.

b. Explain how Anna could find the correct answer.

Name _____

Common Core Standards Practice

3.NF.A.1 Understand a fraction $\frac{1}{b}$ as the quantity formed by 1 part when a whole is partitioned into b equal parts; understand a fraction $\frac{a}{b}$ as the quantity formed by a parts of size $\frac{1}{b}$.

1. Lucy divided the circle into equal parts as shown.

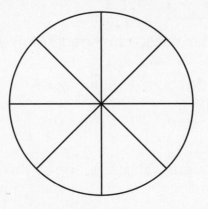

   a. How many equal parts does the circle have?

   b. Shade 5 parts of the circle.

   c. What fraction of the circle is shaded? Tell how you know.

2. Divide the circle into 4 equal parts. Then shade $\frac{1}{4}$.

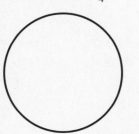

3. What fraction of the circle is shaded?

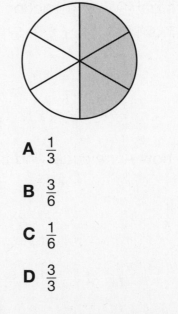

   A $\frac{1}{3}$

   B $\frac{3}{6}$

   C $\frac{1}{6}$

   D $\frac{3}{3}$

CC 25

4. Look at the square below. It is divided into 4 equal parts.

    a. What fraction of the square is each equal part? How do you know?

    b. Shade three parts of the square. What fraction of the square did you shade? How do you know?

5. a. Shade the circle to show $\frac{2}{3}$.

    b. Explain how you showed the fraction $\frac{2}{3}$.

6. Sean divided a circle into 2 equal parts. He shaded 1 part. Write a fraction to name the part Sean shaded.

Name _____

Common Core Standards Practice

3.NF.A.2a Understand a fraction as a number on the number line; represent fractions on a number line diagram.
a. Represent a fraction $\frac{1}{b}$ on a number line diagram by defining the interval from 0 to 1 as the whole and partitioning it into b equal parts. Recognize that each part has size $\frac{1}{b}$ and that the endpoint of the part based at 0 locates the number $\frac{1}{b}$ on the number line.

1. Ella divides the distance between 0 and 1 on a number line into 8 equal parts.

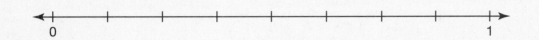

   a. What fraction names the size of each equal part?

   _____

   b. Draw and label the point on the number line that shows $\frac{1}{8}$.

2. Look at the point on the number line.

   a. What fraction does the point show?

   b. Explain how you know.

3. Divide the number line between 0 and 1 into four equal sections. Then draw and label a point to show $\frac{1}{4}$.

   ↤—+————————————————————————+—↦
      0   1

4. a. Draw and label a point to show $\frac{1}{3}$ on the number line.

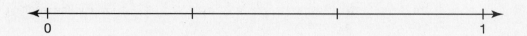

0   1

b. Explain how you knew where to draw the point for $\frac{1}{3}$.

5. a. Divide the number line between 0 and 1 into 2 equal parts.

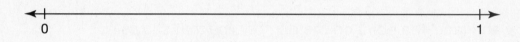

0   1

b. What fraction names the size of each equal part? _____

c. Label the tick mark with the correct fraction.

6. Alana makes a number line from 0 to 1. She uses tick marks to divide it into equal parts.

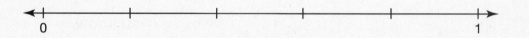

0   1

a. Write a fraction to label the first tick mark to the right of 0.

b. Explain how you knew which fraction to write.

Name _____

Common Core Standards Practice

3.NF.A.2b Understand a fraction as a number on the number line; represent fractions on a number line diagram.
b. Represent a fraction $\frac{a}{b}$ on a number line diagram by marking off a lengths $\frac{1}{b}$ from 0. Recognize that the resulting interval has size $\frac{a}{b}$ and that its endpoint locates the number $\frac{a}{b}$ on the number line.

1. Bridget divides a number line into eight equal parts.

  a. Draw and label a point to show $\frac{5}{8}$.

  b. Explain how you knew where to draw the point for $\frac{5}{8}$.

2. Look at the letters on the number line.

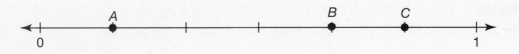

  Which letter on the number line shows $\frac{5}{6}$? Explain how you know.

3. Divide the number line between 0 and 1 into four equal parts. Then draw and label a point to show $\frac{2}{4}$.

4. a. Draw and label a point to show $\frac{3}{4}$ on the number line.

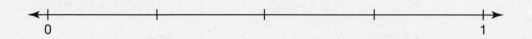

0   1

b. Explain how you knew where to draw the point for $\frac{3}{4}$.

5. a. Divide the number line between 0 and 1 into three equal parts.

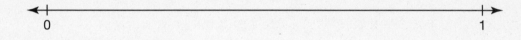

0   1

b. What fraction names the size of each equal part? _____

c. Draw and label a point at $\frac{2}{3}$ on the number line.

6. a. Divide the number line between 0 and 1 into six equal parts.

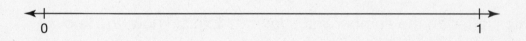

0   1

b. Explain how you used tick marks to show sixths on the number line.

c. Draw and label a point to show $\frac{3}{6}$ on the number line.

Name _____

Common Core Standards Practice

3.NF.A.3a Explain equivalence of fractions in special cases, and compare fractions by reasoning about their size. Understand two fractions as equivalent (equal) if they are the same size, or the same point on a number line.

1. a. Draw and label a point to show $\frac{1}{2}$ on the number line.

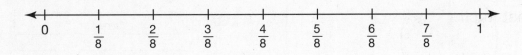

b. What fraction with a denominator of 6 is equal to $\frac{1}{2}$? How do you know?

2. a. Draw and label a point to show $\frac{1}{4}$ on the number line.

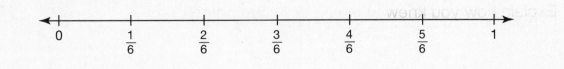

b. What fraction with a denominator of 8 is equal to $\frac{1}{4}$?

3. Grant shaded a circle to show $\frac{1}{2}$.

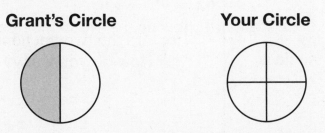

Grant's Circle   **Your Circle**

a. The circle on the right shows fourths. Shade it to show a fraction equal to $\frac{1}{2}$.

b. What fraction with a denominator of 4 is equal to $\frac{1}{2}$?

4. a. Draw and label a point to show $\frac{3}{4}$ on the number line.

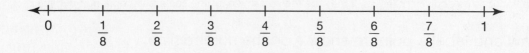

b. Explain how you knew where to draw the point for $\frac{3}{4}$.

c. What fraction with a denominator of 8 is equal to $\frac{3}{4}$?

5. Rachel shaded a circle to show $\frac{4}{6}$.

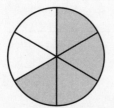

a. Shade the circle below to show a fraction equal to $\frac{4}{6}$.

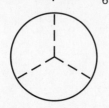

b. What fraction of your circle is shaded?

6. Abby and Will each shaded a fraction of a rectangle.

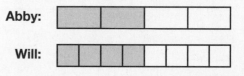

a. What fraction did Abby shade?

b. What fraction did Will shade?

c. Are the two fractions equal? How do you know?

CC 32

Name _____

Common Core Standards Practice

3.NF.A.3b Explain equivalence of fractions in special cases, and compare fractions by reasoning about their size. Recognize and generate simple equivalent fractions, e.g., $\frac{1}{2} = \frac{2}{4}$, $\frac{4}{6} = \frac{2}{3}$. Explain why the fractions are equivalent, e.g., by using a visual fraction model.

1. Which model shows a fraction equivalent to $\frac{3}{6}$?

A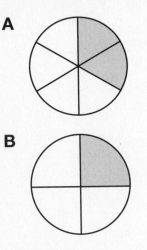

C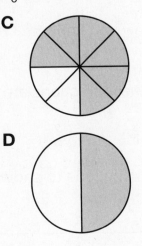

B

D

2. **a.** Which of these fractions are equivalent to $\frac{6}{8}$.

$\frac{4}{6}$ $\qquad$ $\frac{8}{12}$ $\qquad$ $\frac{2}{4}$ $\qquad$ $\frac{3}{4}$ $\qquad$ $\frac{9}{12}$

   b. Draw models to show why the fractions are equivalent.

3. **a.** Name a fraction that is equivalent to $\frac{1}{3}$.

   b. Explain why the fraction you named is equivalent to $\frac{1}{3}$. Use both words and a drawing.

4. a. Which of these fractions are equivalent to $\frac{2}{8}$.

$\frac{3}{12}$ $\qquad$ $\frac{4}{12}$ $\qquad$ $\frac{1}{4}$ $\qquad$ $\frac{2}{4}$ $\qquad$ $\frac{3}{6}$

b. Draw models to show why the fractions are equivalent.

5. a. Which of these fractions are equivalent to $\frac{1}{2}$.

$\frac{4}{6}$ $\qquad$ $\frac{3}{6}$ $\qquad$ $\frac{2}{3}$ $\qquad$ $\frac{2}{4}$ $\qquad$ $\frac{4}{8}$

b. Use the number line to show why the fractions are equivalent.

0   1

6. a. Name a fraction that is equivalent to $\frac{4}{6}$.

b. Explain why the fraction you named is equivalent to $\frac{4}{6}$. Use both words and a drawing.

7. Miguel ate $\frac{2}{4}$ of an apple. April ate an equivalent fraction of an apple. Which could be the fraction that April ate?

A $\frac{2}{8}$

B $\frac{1}{3}$

C $\frac{3}{6}$

D $\frac{3}{4}$

CC 34

Name _____

Common Core Standards Practice

3.NF.A.3c Explain equivalence of fractions in special cases, and compare fractions by reasoning about their size. Express whole numbers as fractions, and recognize fractions that are equivalent to whole numbers.

1. Which fraction is equal to 5?

   A $\frac{1}{5}$

   B $\frac{2}{5}$

   C $\frac{5}{1}$

   D $\frac{5}{5}$

2. Explain how to write the whole number 4 as a fraction.

3. Look at the number line.

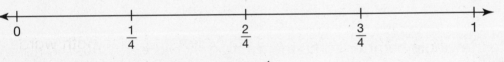

   a. Draw and label a point to show $\frac{4}{4}$.

   b. Explain how you knew where to draw the point for $\frac{4}{4}$.

4. Which letter on the number line shows $\frac{3}{3}$?

5. Mari ate $\frac{2}{2}$ of a peach. What whole number of peaches did Mari eat?

   A 1 peach

   B 2 peaches

   C 3 peaches

   D 4 peaches

6. Which fraction is equal to the whole number 8?

   A $\frac{0}{8}$

   B $\frac{1}{8}$

   C $\frac{8}{1}$

   D $\frac{8}{8}$

7. Look at the number line.

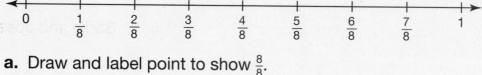

   a. Draw and label point to show $\frac{8}{8}$.

   b. Explain how you knew where to draw the point for $\frac{8}{8}$.

8. Ken wrote the whole number 10 as the fraction $\frac{10}{1}$. Did Ken write the correct fraction for the whole number 10? Explain.

9. Which letter on the number line shows $\frac{6}{6}$?

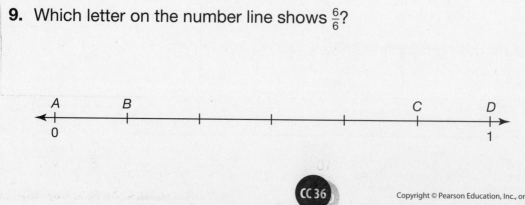

Name _____

Common Core Standards Practice

3.NF.A.3d Explain equivalence of fractions in special cases, and compare fractions by reasoning about their size. Compare two fractions with the same numerator or the same denominator by reasoning about their size. Recognize that comparisons are valid only when the two fractions refer to the same whole. Record the results of comparisons with the symbols >, =, or <, and justify the conclusions, e.g., by using a visual fraction model.

1. **a.** Which fraction is greater, $\frac{2}{6}$ or $\frac{4}{6}$?

   b. Explain how you know which fraction is greater.

2. Sadie ate $\frac{2}{8}$ of a small pizza. Josef ate $\frac{2}{8}$ of a large pizza. Did Sadie and Josef eat the same amount of pizza? Explain.

3. **a.** Which fraction is greater, $\frac{5}{8}$ or $\frac{5}{6}$?

   b. Explain how you know which fraction is greater.

4. Place the fractions below in the appropriate place.

Less than $\frac{1}{2}$	Equal to $\frac{1}{2}$	Greater than $\frac{1}{2}$

$\frac{3}{8}$ $\frac{4}{6}$ $\frac{2}{4}$ $\frac{5}{8}$ $\frac{1}{3}$

$\frac{5}{12}$ $\frac{2}{8}$ $\frac{6}{10}$ $\frac{3}{6}$ $\frac{7}{8}$

CC 37

5. Which fraction is less than $\frac{2}{6}$?

   A $\frac{2}{8}$

   B $\frac{2}{4}$

   C $\frac{3}{6}$

   D $\frac{5}{6}$

6. Circle the smaller fraction.

   $\frac{6}{8}$ $\frac{3}{8}$

7. Ben and Theo each have an orange. The oranges are the same size. Ben eats $\frac{2}{3}$ of his orange. Theo eats $\frac{2}{4}$ of his orange.

   a. Did Ben or Theo eat a larger fraction of the orange?

   b. Draw models of each fraction to show that your answer is correct.

8. a. Which fraction is larger, $\frac{1}{4}$ or $\frac{3}{4}$?

   b. Use the number line to show that your answer is correct.

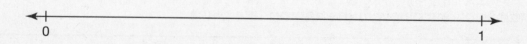

0   1

9. Alonso painted $\frac{1}{2}$ of a large wall. Adele painted $\frac{1}{2}$ of a small wall. Do you think they used the same amount of paint? Explain.

CC 38

Name _____

Common Core Standards Practice

3.MD.A.1 Tell and write time to the nearest minute and measure time intervals in minutes. Solve word problems involving addition and subtraction of time intervals in minutes, e.g., by representing the problem on a number line diagram.

1. Write the time shown on the clock.

_____ : _____

2. Alex leaves for school every day at 8:20. Show this time on the clock below.

3. After school each day, Devin spends 25 minutes on his math homework and 15 minutes on his language arts homework. How many minutes does Devin spend doing his math and language arts homework?

4. Laura goes to lunch at the time shown on the clock. At what time does she go to lunch?

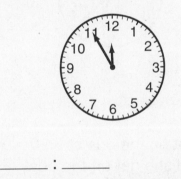

_____ : _____

5. Lily and her parents drove to her grandmother's house. They arrived at her grandmother's house at 9:40 a.m. The drive took 45 minutes. At what time did Lily and her parents leave their house?

  a. Model this problem on the number line.

  ←┼──┼──┼──┼──┼──┼──┼──┼──┼──┼──┼──┼→

  b. Tell what time Lily and her parents left their house.

6. Tristan's math class starts at 1:37. Draw hands on the clock to show 1:37.

7. A play ended at 7:30. It began 1 hour and 10 minutes earlier. At what time did the play begin?

_____ : _____

8. What time does the clock show?

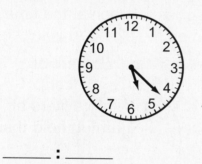

_____ : _____

9. After school, Marta and her sister play one game for 45 minutes. Then they play another game for 30 minutes. For how long did Marta and her sister play games?

10. Julia got on the bus at 2:20 P.M. She got off the bus 50 minutes later. At what time did she get off the bus?

a. Model this problem on the number line.

b. Tell what time Julie got off the bus.

Name _____

Common Core Standards Practice

3.MD.A.2 Measure and estimate liquid volumes and masses of objects using standard units of grams (g), kilograms (kg), and liters (l). Add, subtract, multiply, or divide to solve one-step word problems involving masses or volumes that are given in the same units, e.g., by using drawings (such as a beaker with a measurement scale) to represent the problem.

1. Which is the best estimate of the capacity of the pitcher?

  A 1 liter

  B 5 liters

  C 10 liters

  D 100 liters

2. Mr. Roberts went to the farmer's market on Wednesday and bought 450 grams of ground beef and 600 grams of ground pork. How much meat did Mr. Robert buy on Wednesday?

  A 250 grams

  B 510 grams

  C 1,050 grams

  D 1,150 grams

3. Circle the best estimate for the mass of the pillow.

  1 kg   10 kg   100 kg

4. A bathtub holds 150 liters of water. A sink holds 12 liters of water. How many more liters of water does the bathtub hold than the sink?

5. Ryan has 2 apples. One has a mass of 130 grams. The other has a mass of 124 grams. What is the combined mass of the two apples?

6. How many liters of water are in the bucket?

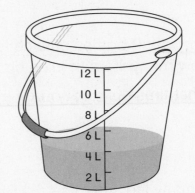

7. A bag of food has a mass of 20 kilograms. A worker at a zoo uses all of the food in the bag to feed 10 animals. She gives each animal an equal share of the food. How many kilograms of food does each animal get?

A 2 kilograms

B 10 kilograms

C 30 kilograms

D 200 kilograms

9. What is the mass of the tomatoes on the scale?

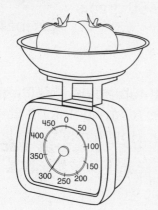

8. Circle the best estimate for the mass of the bowling ball.

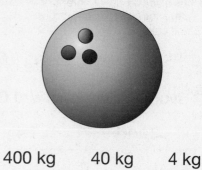

400 kg   40 kg   4 kg

10. In science class, Ashton put 150 milliliters of oil in the beaker. Then he put 50 milliliters of vinegar into the same beaker.

a. On the beaker below, show the amount of oil and vinegar Ashton put in the beaker.

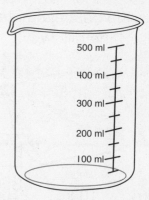

b. How many milliliters of liquid did Ashton put in the beaker?

11. Blanca bought 9 bottles of juice for a party. Each bottle holds 2 liters of juice. How many liters of juice did Blanca buy?

a. What operation do you need to use to solve the problem? Explain why?

b. How many liters of juice did Blanca buy?

Name _____

Common Core Standards Practice

3.MD.B.3 Draw a scaled picture graph and a scaled bar graph to represent a data set with several categories. Solve one- and two-step "how many more" and "how many less" problems using information presented in scaled bar graphs.

1. Use the information in the tally chart to complete the picture graph.

Favorite Sports of Third Graders

Sport	Tally
Baseball	卌 l
Football	卌 lll
Soccer	卌 卌 ll

Favorite Sports of Third Graders

Baseball	
Football	
Soccer	
Key:	stands for 2 students

How many more students picked soccer as their favorite sport than baseball? Tell how you know.

The picture graph below shows how the third-grade students at a school get to school each day. Use the picture graph for questions 2 and 3.

Ways to Get to School

Bus	✪ ✪ ✪ ✪ ✪
Bike	✪
Walk	✪ ✪
Car	✪ ✪ ✪ ✪
Key: ✪ stands for 6 students	

2. How many fewer students walk to school than ride in a car?

3. How many more students take the bus to school than walk or bike?

 CC 43

4. The table shows the number of laps that 4 students swam last week. Use the information in the table to complete the bar graph.

Name	Laps
Molly	50
Fred	40
Jessica	45
Mateo	30

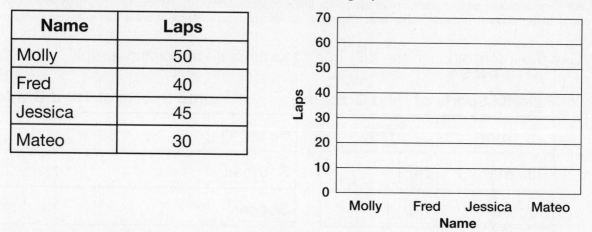

The bar graph below shows the number of some of the animals at a zoo. Use the bar graph for questions 5 and 6.

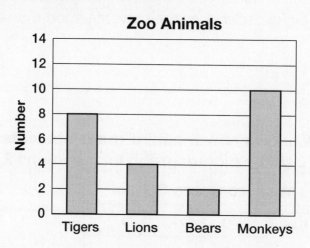

5. How many fewer bears than tigers are at the zoo?

6. Lions and tigers are large cats. How many more large cats than monkeys are at the zoo?

CC 44

Name _____

Common Core Standards Practice

3.MD.B.4 Generate measurement data by measuring lengths using rulers marked with halves and fourths of an inch. Show the data by making a line plot, where the horizontal scale is marked off in appropriate units—whole numbers, halves, or quarters.

1. The list below shows the lengths of the snakes at a pet store. Display the data in a line plot.

Snake Lengths (inches)					
$6\frac{1}{2}$	7	$7\frac{1}{4}$	$6\frac{3}{4}$	$6\frac{3}{4}$	$7\frac{1}{2}$
$6\frac{3}{4}$	$6\frac{1}{2}$	$7\frac{1}{2}$	$7\frac{1}{4}$	$6\frac{3}{4}$	$7\frac{1}{4}$

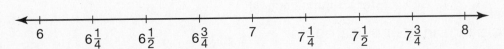

$$6 \qquad 6\frac{1}{4} \qquad 6\frac{1}{2} \qquad 6\frac{3}{4} \qquad 7 \qquad 7\frac{1}{4} \qquad 7\frac{1}{2} \qquad 7\frac{3}{4} \qquad 8$$

2. Find 6 pencils in your classroom.

   a. Use a ruler to measure each pencil to the nearest fourth of an inch. Write the length of each pencil below.

   b. Use the lengths of the pencils to complete the line plot.

Pencil Lengths (inches)

3. The list below shows the lengths of Aaron's toy cars. Use the information to complete the line plot.

Car Lengths (inches)				
1	$1\frac{3}{4}$	2	$1\frac{1}{2}$	2
1	$1\frac{1}{2}$	2	2	1

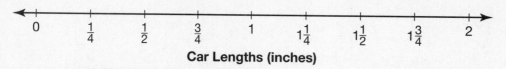

Car Lengths (inches)

4. Find 6 crayons in your classroom.

    a. Use a ruler to measure each crayon to the nearest fourth of an inch. Write the length of each crayon below.

    b. Use the lengths of the crayons to complete the line plot.

Crayon Lengths (inches)

Name _____

Common Core Standards Practice

3.MD.C.5a Recognize area as an attribute of plane figures and understand concepts of area measurement. A square with side length 1 unit, called "a unit square," is said to have "one square unit" of area, and can be used to measure area.
3.MD.C.5b Recognize area as an attribute of plane figures and understand concepts of area measurement. A plane figure which can be covered without gaps or overlaps by *n* unit squares is said to have an area of *n* square units.

1. Alicia is to find the area of this rectangle. She has some inch squares. Tell her what to do to find the area.

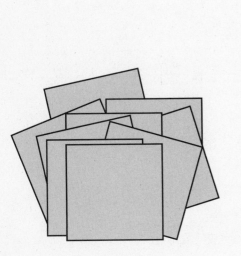

2. Hudson completely covers a rectangle with unit squares as shown below. What is the area of the rectangle? How do you know?

3. Which of these objects can Milly use to find the area of a square? Explain your answer.

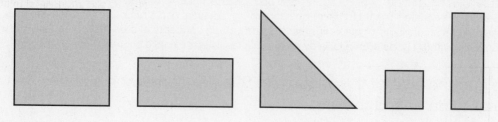

4. Cassie has a new rug in her bedroom. The rug is 9 square feet. Draw a model of Cassie's new rug. Show that it is 9 square feet.

5. Circle the units used to measure area.

feet	square inches	centimeters
square meters	square feet	meters

Name _____

Common Core Standards Practice

3.MD.C.6 Measure areas by counting unit squares (square cm, square m, square in, square ft, and improvised units).

1. What is the area of the rectangle below?

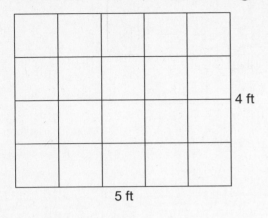

4 ft

5 ft

2. Explain how you found the area of the rectangle.

Find the area of each figure. Be sure to use the correct units.

3.

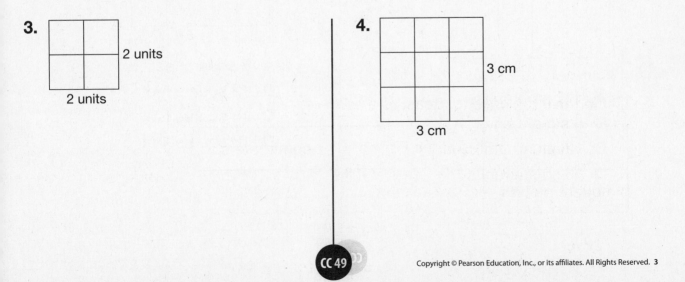

2 units

2 units

4.

3 cm

3 cm

Find the area of each figure. Be sure to use the correct units.

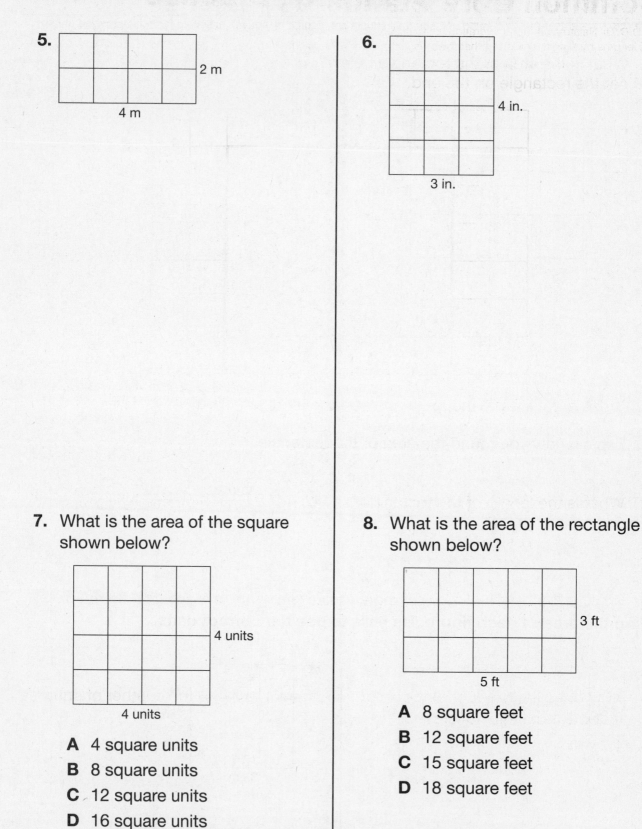

5.

2 m

4 m

6.

4 in.

3 in.

7. What is the area of the square shown below?

4 units

4 units

A 4 square units

B 8 square units

C 12 square units

D 16 square units

8. What is the area of the rectangle shown below?

3 ft

5 ft

A 8 square feet

B 12 square feet

C 15 square feet

D 18 square feet

CC 50

3

Name _____

Common Core Standards Practice

3.MD.C.7a Relate area to the operations of multiplication and addition. Find the area of a rectangle with whole-number side lengths by tiling it, and show that the area is the same as would be found by multiplying the side lengths.

Look at the rectangle on the grid.

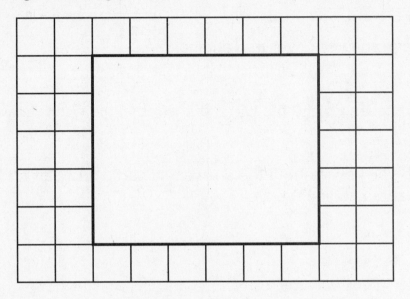

1. What is the area of the rectangle above? Tell how you know.

2. What is the length of the rectangle above? Tell how you determined the length.

3. What is the height of the rectangle above? Tell how you determined the height.

4. How does the product of the length and height relate to the number of squares that the rectangle covers?

5. Look at the rectangle below.

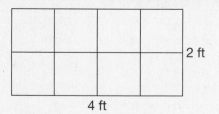

4 ft

a. How many squares cover the rectangle?

b. Multiply the length and the width of the rectangle. What answer do you get?

c. What do you notice about the answers in part a and part b? What does that tell you about finding the area?

6. a. Give two different ways to find the area of the square.

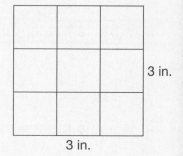

b. Use both ways to find the area of the square.

First way: Area =

Second way: Area =

c. Do you get the same answer? Why?

Name _____

Common Core Standards Practice

3.MD.C.7b Relate area to the operations of multiplication and addition. **b.** Multiply side lengths to find areas of rectangles with whole-number side lengths in the context of solving real world and mathematical problems, and represent whole-number products as rectangular areas in mathematical reasoning.

Find the area of each square or rectangle.

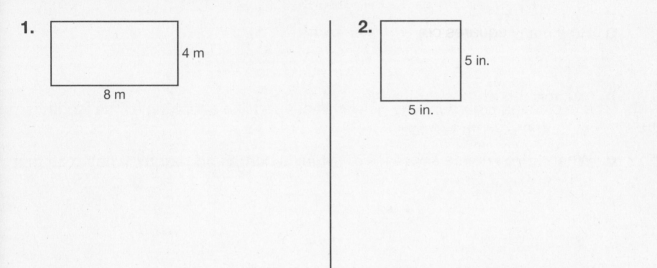

1.

4 m

8 m

2.

5 in.

5 in.

3. A rug is shaped like a rectangle. The length of the rug is 9 feet, and the width is 6 feet. What is the area of the rug?

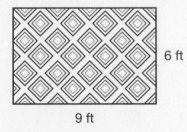

6 ft

9 ft

   A 30 square ft

   B 15 square ft

   C 54 square ft

   D 63 square ft

4. Ms. Leonard plans to put square tiles on her kitchen floor. Each tile covers 1 square foot and costs $1. How much will the tiles for the floor cost?

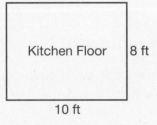

Kitchen Floor   8 ft

10 ft

CC 53

5. Troy wants to make a pen for his rabbits. The pen will be a rectangle with an area of 24 square meters. Answer Yes or No if the length and width could be the dimensions of Troy's rabbit pen.

A length: 2 m, width: 6 m   YES   NO

B length: 3 m, width: 8 m   YES   NO

C length: 5 m, width: 5 m   YES   NO

D length: 4 m, width: 6 m   YES   NO

6. Izzie is planting a garden. Her garden is shaped like a rectangle. The length is 7 feet, and the width is 3 feet.

   a. Draw a picture of Izzie's garden. Label the length and width.

   b. What is the area of Izzie's garden?

     Area =

7. The drawing shows the lid of a box. Lorrie is gluing square tiles to the lid. Each tile has an area of 1 square centimeter.

   a. How many tiles will Lorrie need to completely cover the lid?

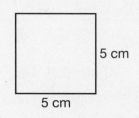

5 cm

5 cm

   b. Explain how you found your answer.

3

Name _____

Common Core Standards Practice

3.MD.C.7c Relate area to the operations of multiplication and addition. Use tiling to show in a concrete case that the area of a rectangle with whole-number side lengths *a* and *b* + *c* is the sum of *a* × *b* and *a* × *c*. Use area models to represent the distributive property in mathematical reasoning.

1. Max drew a model of his garden. He has one part for vegetables and one part for herbs.

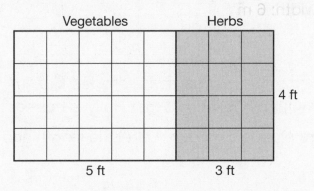

a. What is the area of the part of the garden for vegetables?

b. What is the area of the part of the garden for herbs?

c. What is the area of the garden?

2. Ralph's father will put new tiles on the kitchen floor. Ralph draws a model of the kitchen floor. What is the area of the kitchen floor?

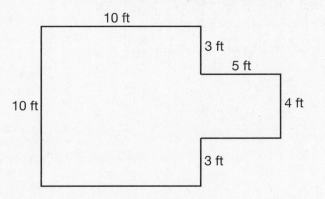

3. Holly says that 3×9 is the same as the sum of 3×5 and 3×4.

    a. On the grid below, draw a model to show that Holly is correct.

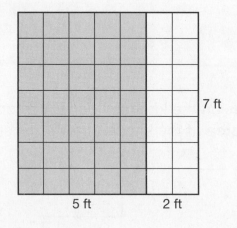

    b. Explain how your model shows that Holly is correct.

4. How does the model below show that 7×7 is the same as $(7 \times 5) + (7 \times 2)$?

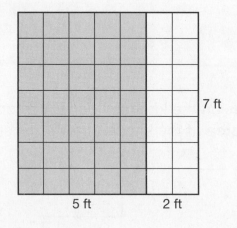

7 ft

5 ft   2 ft

Name _____

Common Core Standards Practice

3.MD.C.7d Relate area to the operations of multiplication and addition. Recognize area as additive. Find areas of rectilinear figures by decomposing them into non-overlapping rectangles and adding the areas of the non-overlapping parts, applying this technique to solve real world problems.

1. Linda's bedroom floor has side lengths of 12 feet and 9 feet. She drew a picture of the floor, and then broke it apart into two smaller rectangles.

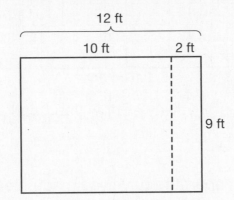

   a. What is the area of each smaller rectangle?

   b. What is the total area of the floor? How do you know?

2. Curt made a bookmark in the shape of a rectangle. The bookmark has a length of 15 centimeters and a width of 5 centimeters.

   a. Break apart the bookmark into two smaller rectangles to make it easier to find the area.

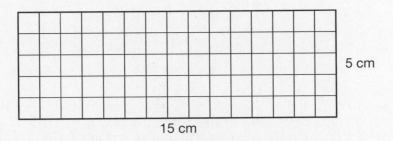

   b. What is the area of the bookmark? Show your work.

3. A driveway has the shape of a rectangle. It is 16 meters long and 4 meters wide.

    a. Break apart the driveway into two smaller rectangles to make it easier to find the area.

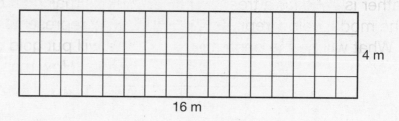

16 m

    b. What is the area of the driveway? Show your work.

    c. Explain how breaking apart the driveway made it easier to find the area.

4. A mirror has the shape of a rectangle. It is 13 inches long and 6 inches wide. What is the area of the mirror? Show your work.

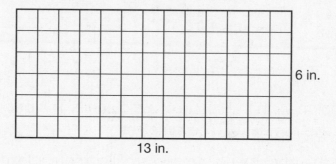

13 in.

Name _____

Common Core Standards Practice

3.MD.D.8 Solve real world and mathematical problems involving perimeters of polygons, including finding the perimeter given the side lengths, finding an unknown side length, and exhibiting rectangles with the same perimeter and different areas or with the same area and different perimeters.

1. Harry's father is building a tree house. The model below represents the floor. What will be the perimeter of the floor?

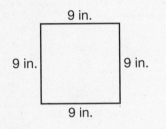

Perimeter = _____

2. Ama is making a banner. The model below represents her banner. She will put gold cord around the banner. How many centimeters of gold cord will she use?

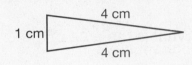

Perimeter = _____

3. The perimeter of the triangle is 9 centimeters. What is the missing side length?

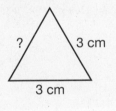

4. The perimeter of the figure is 20 inches. What is the missing side length?

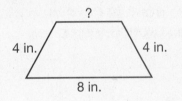

5. The drawing shows the yard of the Lang family. What is the perimeter of the yard?

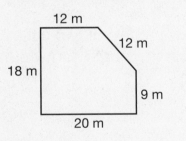

6. Look at the rectangle shown below.

   a. What are the perimeter and area of the rectangle?

     Perimeter = _____   Area = _____

   b. On the grid, draw a rectangle that has the same perimeter, but a different area.

   c. What is the area of the rectangle you drew?

7. A farmer needs to build a new animal corral in the shape of a rectangle. The pen needs to have an area of 72 square meters. He will need to buy fencing to go around the corral.

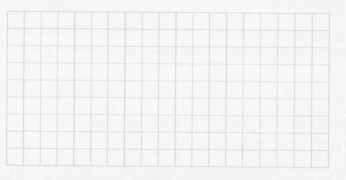

   a. What could be the dimensions of the corral? Draw models of two different rectangles with an area of 72 square meters. Label the length and width of each model.

   b. Which of your models will require more fencing? Tell how you know.

Name _____

Common Core Standards Practice

3.G.A.1 Understand that shapes in different categories (e.g., rhombuses, rectangles, and others) may share attributes (e.g., having four sides), and that the shared attributes can define a larger category (e.g., quadrilaterals). Recognize rhombuses, rectangles, and squares as examples of quadrilaterals, and draw examples of quadrilaterals that do not belong to any of these subcategories.

1. What are two ways these shapes are alike?

2. Circle the shapes that have 4 sides and exactly 2 right angles.

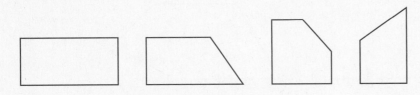

3. Which of these shapes appears to be a rhombus?

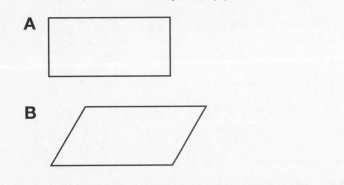 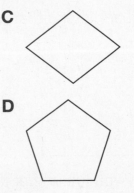

A

C

B

D

4. Which of these quadrilaterals is NOT a rectangle?

A

C

B

D

5. a. Draw a quadrilateral that is not a rhombus, a square, or a rectangle.

b. Explain how you know that your quadrilateral is not a rhombus, a square, or a rectangle.

6. What is one way these shapes are alike?

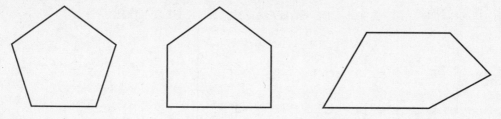

7. a. Circle the quadrilateral that appears to be a square.

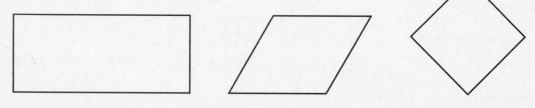

b. Explain how you know that the quadrilateral you picked is a square.

Name _____

Common Core Standards Practice

3.G.A.2 Partition shapes into parts with equal areas. Express the area of each part as a unit fraction of the whole.

1. The rectangle is divided into 4 equal parts. What fraction of the area of the rectangle is the area of each part?

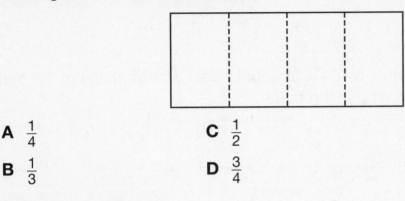

   A $\frac{1}{4}$ **C** $\frac{1}{2}$

   B $\frac{1}{3}$ **D** $\frac{3}{4}$

2. Look at the hexagon.

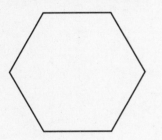

   a. Divide the hexagon into 6 equal parts.

   b. What fraction of the area of the hexagon is the area of each part?

3. **a.** Show three different ways you can divide a square into 2 equal parts.

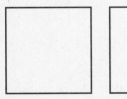 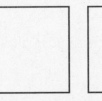

   b. What fraction of the area of the square is the area of each part?

4. Look at the circle.

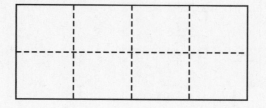

    a. Divide the circle into equal parts so that the area of each part is $\frac{1}{4}$ of the area of the circle.

    b. Into how many equal parts did you divide the circle?

5. Brian divided the rectangle below into equal parts. What fraction of the area of the rectangle is the area of each part?

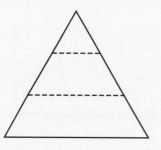

6. Ella divided a triangle into 3 parts as shown below.

    a. Ella says that the area of each part is $\frac{1}{3}$ of the area of the triangle. Explain why Ella is incorrect.

    b. Divide the triangle below into 3 parts so that the area of each part is $\frac{1}{3}$ of the total area.

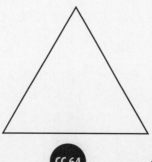

Name _____

Practice End-of-Year Assessment

1. The bar graph shows the favorite pets of the third grade.

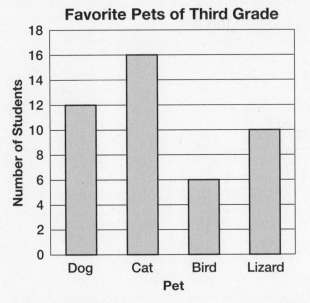

Favorite Pets of Third Grade

How many more students chose dogs or cats than chose birds?

....

2. **a.** Name a fraction equivalent to $\frac{1}{4}$.

b. Draw models to show why the fractions are equivalent.

3. Sara buys 6 pencils with a $20 bill. Each pencil costs $2.

    a. How much change should Sara receive?

    b. Explain how you found your answer.

....

4. Which of these numbers round to 1,780 when rounded to the nearest ten? Circle all that apply.

1,784	1,874	1,775
1,708	1,779	1,799

....

5. There are 3 rows of cans. Each row has 4 cans.

    a. Draw an array to show how many cans there are in all.

    b. How many cans are there in all?

6. Divide the number line into three equal parts. Then draw and label a point to show $\frac{1}{3}$.

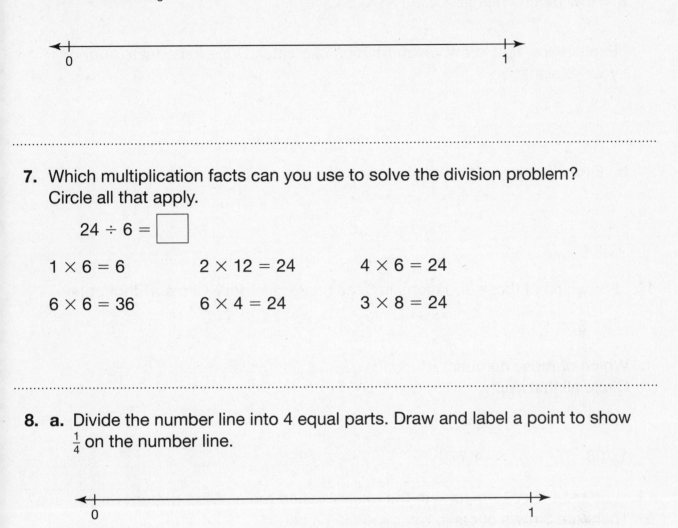

7. Which multiplication facts can you use to solve the division problem? Circle all that apply.

$24 \div 6 = \boxed{}$

$1 \times 6 = 6$ $2 \times 12 = 24$ $4 \times 6 = 24$

$6 \times 6 = 36$ $6 \times 4 = 24$ $3 \times 8 = 24$

8. a. Divide the number line into 4 equal parts. Draw and label a point to show $\frac{1}{4}$ on the number line.

b. Explain how you knew where to draw the point for $\frac{1}{4}$.

9. Compare the fractions. Write $>$, $=$, or $<$.

$$\frac{1}{5} \underline{\hspace{1cm}} \frac{1}{9}$$

Explain how you know which fraction is greater. Draw a model to support your explanation.

....

10. For which of these equations is 3 the missing factor? Circle all that apply.

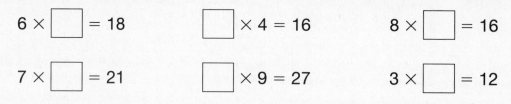

$6 \times \boxed{} = 18$ $\qquad$ $\boxed{} \times 4 = 16$ $\qquad$ $8 \times \boxed{} = 16$

$7 \times \boxed{} = 21$ $\qquad$ $\boxed{} \times 9 = 27$ $\qquad$ $3 \times \boxed{} = 12$

....

11. Look at the column for 4 in the multiplication table. What pattern do you see?

X	0	1	2	3	4	5	6
0	0	0	0	0	0	0	0
1	0	1	2	3	4	5	6
2	0	2	4	6	8	10	12
3	0	3	6	9	12	15	18
4	0	4	8	12	16	20	24
5	0	5	10	15	20	25	30
6	0	6	12	18	24	30	36

CC 68

12. Leo needs 4 pieces of tape, each 5 inches long.

    a. Write an equation to show how much tape Leo needs in all. Use the letter *t* to stand for the missing number.

    b. How many inches of tape does Leo need in all?

---

13. Baseball practice ended at 4:10. It began 30 minutes earlier. Which shows when baseball practice began?

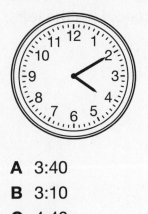

    A 3:40

    B 3:10

    C 4:40

    D 3:50

---

14. Tell how to find 4×9 by breaking apart 9 into $5 + 4$. You can use words or models.

15. A cook makes 3 pots of soup. Each pot holds 8 liters of soup. How many liters of soup did the cook make in all?

16. Look at the numbers in the table. What pattern do you see?

4	9	14	19	24

17. There are 28 people going on a boat ride. Each boat can hold 4 people.

    a. Write an equation to show how many boats they will need. Use the letter *b* to stand for the missing number.

    b. How many boats will they need?

18. What is the area of the rectangle? Be sure to use the correct units.

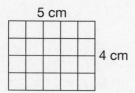

19. A fish has a mass of 26 kilograms. The mass of a turtle is 8 kilograms less than the mass of the fish. What is the mass of the turtle?

20. **a.** What is the missing number in the equation?

$$9 \times 8 = \boxed{} \times 9$$

b. Explain how you know.

21. **a.** Write a word problem that matches $12 \div 4$.

b. Explain why your problem matches $12 \div 4$.

22. A third grade class is growing bean plants. The list below shows the heights of the plants. Use the information to complete the line plot.

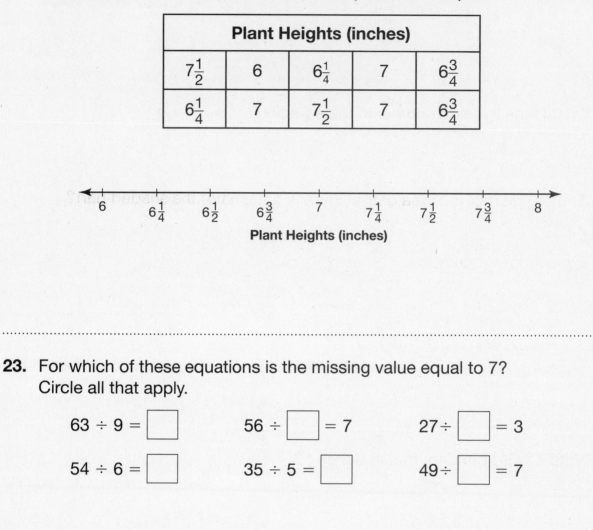

Plant Heights (inches)				
$7\frac{1}{2}$	6	$6\frac{1}{4}$	7	$6\frac{3}{4}$
$6\frac{1}{4}$	7	$7\frac{1}{2}$	7	$6\frac{3}{4}$

6    $6\frac{1}{4}$ $6\frac{1}{2}$ $6\frac{3}{4}$ 7 $7\frac{1}{4}$ $7\frac{1}{2}$ $7\frac{3}{4}$ 8

Plant Heights (inches)

23. For which of these equations is the missing value equal to 7? Circle all that apply.

$63 \div 9 = \boxed{}$ $56 \div \boxed{} = 7$ $27 \div \boxed{} = 3$

$54 \div 6 = \boxed{}$ $35 \div 5 = \boxed{}$ $49 \div \boxed{} = 7$

24. Write the time shown on the clock.

_____ : _____

25. **a.** Divide the figure into 8 equal parts. Then shade one of the parts.

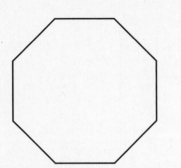

b. What fraction of the area of the figure is the area of the shaded part?

26. What is the area of the rectangle?

3 units

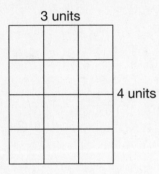

4 units

27. Which number makes the equation true?

$$48 \div \boxed{} = 8$$

A 8

B 7

C 6

D 9

28. The perimeter of the figure is 18 feet.

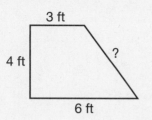

   a. What is the missing side length?

   b. Tell how you know.

---

29. For each equation in 29a–29d, answer Yes or No if the ☐ = 8 makes the equation true.

   a. $4 \times$ ☐ $= 32$ YES   NO

   b. ☐ $\times 6 = 56$ YES   NO

   c. $5 \times$ ☐ $= 40$ YES   NO

   d. ☐ $\times 8 = 56$ YES   NO

---

30. Ms. Carr has a flowerbed in the shape of a rectangle. The flowerbed has a length of 14 feet and a width of 4 feet.

   a. Break apart the flowerbed into two smaller rectangles to make it easier to find the area.

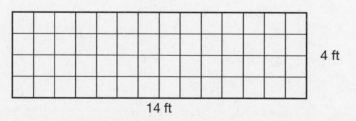

   b. What is the area of the flowerbed? Show your work.

31. How can the product of 6 and 7 help you find the product of 60 and 7?

....

32. Write a multiplication fact that can help you solve the division problem.

$36 \div 9 = \boxed{}$

....

33. A door is shaped liked a rectangle. The length of the door is 7 feet, and the width is 3 feet. What is the area of the door?

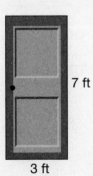

7 ft

3 ft

34. a. Divide the rectangle into 3 equal parts. Shade 1 of the parts.

b. What fraction of the rectangle is shaded?

....

35. Which quadrilateral does NOT have any square corners?

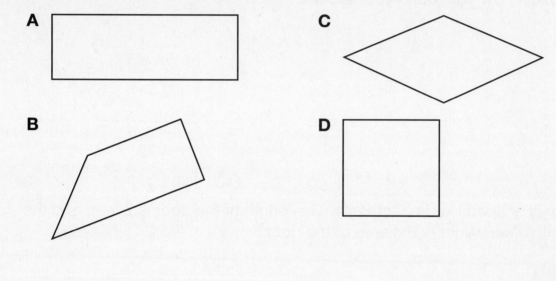

A

C

B

D

....

36. A flag has an area of 12 square feet. Explain what this sentence means.

37. Multiply.

$$
\begin{array}{r}
9 \\
\times\ 5 \\
\hline
\end{array}
$$

38. Erin had 28 cards. She kept 8 for herself. She shared the rest equally between her 2 brothers.

    a. How many cards did each of Erin's brothers get?

    b. Explain how you found your answer.

39. Subtract.

$$
\begin{array}{r}
326 \\
-\ \ 38 \\
\hline
\end{array}
$$

40. Mr. Padilla has 3 apples. He cuts each apple into 8 pieces. He puts 4 apple pieces into each bag.

    a. How many bags will Mr. Padilla need?

    b. Explain how you found your answer.

CC 77

Name _____

Performance Task 1

Raising Funds

Part A

The students in Ms. Jansen's third grade class are having a school bake sale. They want to raise $500 for a fieldtrip.

Ms. Jansen asked her students' families to volunteer to bring in brownies, cookies, or large cupcakes for the sale.

From the volunteer sign-up sheets, Ms. Jansen determines they will have 80 large cupcakes and 240 brownies for the bake sale. Nobody signed up to bring in cookies yet.

The students decide that they will sell the large cupcakes for $2 each, and brownies and cookies for $1 each.

1. How much money can the students make if they sell all of the cupcakes and brownies?

2. How many cookies will be needed for the class to reach their goal of $500?

3. How many families will need to volunteer to bring cookies, if each family brings 20 cookies?

Part B

The bake sale will take place from 11:00 to 12:00 every school day for one week. The students will set up tables outside the school lunchroom and will invite teachers, students, and parents to the bake sale.

Ms. Jansen has decided to have 30-minute shifts for the bake sale. Two students will work at each shift.

4. How many shifts will each of the 20 students in the class have to work during the week-long bake sale?

Name _____

Performance Task 2

A Nature Hike

Part A

Colton and Rashad are hiking a trail to a waterfall in a nature preserve. After hiking for 30 minutes, they see the sign below.

Rashad says, "Half-way? Is that all? That's less than $\frac{1}{3}$ of the trail."

Colton disagrees. He says, "$\frac{1}{2}$ of the trail is greater than $\frac{1}{3}$ of the trail."

1. Who is correct? Use two different models to show whether Rashad or Colton is correct.

Part B

Colton and Rashad each have a water bottle for the hike. When they began the hike, their water bottles were full. Their water bottles are shown below.

Colton's Water Bottle   **Rashad's Water Bottle**

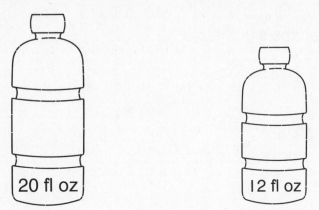

20 fl oz   12 fl oz

When they get to the waterfall, Colton says, "My water bottle is half empty."

Rashad looks at his water bottle and says, "Mine is, too. But you have more water left than I do." Colton answers, "How can I have more water? Both of our bottles are half empty."

2. Why does Rashad say that Colton has more water left in his bottle than he does?

3. How can Rashad show Colton that he is correct? Explain what Rashad can do.

CC 81